D0886547

MARY CASSATT

The Life and Art of a Genteel Rebel

by Cos Ferrara

Mary Cassatt The Life and Art of a Genteel Rebel, Copyright, © 2004 by Girls Explore™ LLC

Library of Congress Control Number: 2004114153

ISBN 0-9749456-3-3

Printed in the United States of America
10 9 8 7 6 5 4 3 2 1

Photo Credits:

Chapter Photo Portrait of Mary Cassatt, Ca 1914, original has been cropped. Research Material on Mary Cassatt and James A. McNeill Whistler, 1872-1975, Archives of American Art, Smithsonian Institution

Cover Photo:
Self Portrait by Mary Cassatt, 1880
© Geoffrey Clements/CORBIS

Cover Design - Chris Kelley – Jon Reis Photo + Design
Interior Design – Vernon Thornblad PoGo Studio

CONTENTS

Self-Portrait by Mary Cassatt The Metropolitan Museum of Art,
Bequest of Edith H. Proskauer, 1975.
(1975.319.1) Photograph © 1998 The Metropolitan Museum of Art.

I

Introduction

Imagine how you would feel if you went to a park and saw the sign: "No girls allowed." Or suppose you wanted to be a doctor, or police officer, or airplane pilot, and you were told: "Sorry. Boys only." You'd probably feel very angry.

Well, that's how Mary Cassatt felt throughout much of her life. Since the time she was a young teenager, people were telling her "No," just because she was a woman.

Today you enjoy many more opportunities than Mary did. For instance, if you work hard enough, you can enter any profession you want to. Mary could not. In fact, her family was outraged when she announced she wanted a career. When Mary said she wanted to be a painter, they were shocked. The art world was dominated completely by men. But Mary did not think it had to be that way.

Because Mary—and other women like her—would not just "go away," you have the chance to be anything you want to be. Instead of just accepting the unfair "Girls are not allowed" signs, those women persisted. Eventually they won.

Many of those women worked for equal rights by forming large groups. They protested. They wrote papers. They marched in parades. They did all they could to call attention to injustice.

Others, like Mary, worked independently and quietly. Mary let her painting do most of her talking. She just continued to paint until people could no longer ignore the quality of her work.

In her work, Mary also broke down barriers. For years people had been taught to paint in only one way. Mary had different ideas. Eventually people saw the brilliance in Mary's style. Today her paintings are recognized worldwide.

As you read about this courageous woman who lived a century ago, you'll see an example of someone who knew her own mind. She was determined but tried not to be disagreeable. She went along with the established patterns—for a time. She followed the traditions of painting—to a point. Ultimately, though, she had to make choices. Would she take the easy path that everyone else took? Or would she follow her heart?

Read on to see the choices that Mary made. See how she made those choices. Her life story can help you some day when you have to make choices of your own.

I

"I Want to Be an Artist"

The Cassatt household was abuzz. Everyone in the family was preparing for the trip. Seven year-old Mary Stevenson Cassatt was excited. She had been on trips before. But this one was special. The family would be leaving the United States. They would be going to Paris, France—for four years.

Mary was looking forward to sailing across the Atlantic Ocean. She had heard much about the beauty of Paris and couldn't wait to see it. But she was also fearful.

She'd be leaving her friends in Pennsylvania. She'd be going to a new school—where everyone spoke French. "What will it be like?" she probably wondered. "How will I get along in a school where kids don't speak English?"

Mary was born in 1844 in Allegheny City, just outside of Pittsburgh, Pennsylvania. Her father, Robert Cassatt, was for a time the city's mayor. He was also a successful businessman and quite wealthy. He filled the Cassatt home with expensive furniture and carpeting as well as portraits of the family members.[1]

The lady of the house was Mary's mother, Katherine. She was a talented and educated woman. Mrs. Cassatt encouraged her children to be interested in learning, to study hard, and to develop their talents. Mary took that encouragement to heart.

Mary had one sister and three brothers. Lydia was the oldest; she was seven years older than Mary. Her brother Alexander was five years older. (The family called him Aleck.) Then came Robert. Robbie was two years older than Mary. Mary was next in line, followed by Gardner. Gard was born five years after Mary.[2]

The Cassatt children attended private schools. But Mr. Cassatt felt that schools could teach children only so much. He wanted his children to learn the things that could be learned only through travel. And the best place to travel to for this kind of learning was Europe. Because his ancestors were French, Mr. Cassatt thought the best place for his children would be Paris, France.[3]

So, in 1851, when Mary was seven years old, the Cassatt family boarded an ocean liner. Paris would be their home for the next four years.

Mary was enrolled in a French school. With the help of a tutor, she quickly learned to speak French.

According to plan, Mary's parents wasted no time in showing her the places and things for which they had come to France. Mary enjoyed them all. She loved going to the theater and ballet with her parents, brothers, and sister. She became a skilled rider by riding horses in a nearby park. The family bought clothes of the latest fashions in the most chic shops of Paris. Mary went along on these shopping trips. Even more than the shops, Mary loved the art galleries. There were so many. Mary never tired of looking at the lovely sculptures and paintings.

Though their home was in Paris, the Cassatt family took many trips outside France. They visited Germany, England, Italy, and Spain. In each country and city, Mary learned about the place's history. She came to know the local customs and attitudes. She enjoyed the different foods, music, and art.[4]

Mary drank in all of the sights and sounds. Besides learning to speak French fluently, she also could hold a conversation in Italian and Spanish. She absorbed the manners of refined members of European society. Mr. Cassatt's plan to truly educate Mary was a success. What he had not planned on, though, was Mary's becoming more interested in art than he would have liked.

Photograph of a drawing of the Cassatt children with their father by Baumgaertner, ca. 1854. Research material on Mary Cassatt and James A. McNeill Whistler, 1872-1975, Archives of American Art, Smithsonian Institution

Why did Mary become so interested in art while in Europe? Hadn't she seen art at home? Not much. At that time—1851—the United States was only 75 years old. That's very young for a country. And the people in the United States were busy building the country. They didn't have much time for the finer things of life, like art and music. But France, Italy, England, Spain, and Germany were hundreds of years older. Their people had had a big head start developing musicians, sculptors, and painters. While the United States had a few museums, Europe offered many. The art collections in the United States were small; in Europe they were large. Most of the great works of art were housed in Europe–in France, Italy, and Spain. The Cassatts took advantage of all that these countries had to offer.

After four years, the family returned home to the United States. Mary was then 11 years old. They moved a number of times. From Allegheny City, they moved to a country home near Lancaster, Pennsylvania. A few years later they moved to Philadelphia. Mary adapted to living as an American in the United States. But she did not forget her European experience.

Mary Tells Her Parents

While in high school, Mary decided that she wanted a career. That idea was practically unheard of at that time. Young women from wealthy families didn't have careers. They were expected to marry wealthy young men and raise children. The education these women received would be used in rearing their children properly. There was no thought of a woman's being schooled for a career in business, law, or science. That was only for young men.

But Mary didn't think that way. She wanted to be independent. She wanted to develop a skill so she could support herself. She did not want to have to depend on her father—or a husband—for her livelihood.

When Mary revealed her thinking to her parents, they were shocked. Even her mother was surprised. Mrs. Cassatt was considered a "modern" woman at the time.

She kept up with the news of the world and current affairs. (Mary later painted a picture of her mother reading a newspaper.) She was all for educating the children—including the girls. But she thought Mary's desire for a career was totally unwise.

Mary, however, did not back down. In fact, she took her argument one step further. Not only did she want a career; but she also told her parents she wanted to be a professional artist. She would support herself painting pictures—the kind she had seen in Europe.

It's easy to imagine the wrangling that went on in the Cassatt household that day. Here was Mr. Cassatt, a leader in business and a former mayor. He was strong-willed and used to having his way. Here was 16-year old Mary, defying him. And here was Mrs. Cassatt, trying to calm her husband and talk some sense into Mary. The conversation may have gone something like this.

Mary: "I want to have a career."

Mr. Cassatt: "Nonsense, Dear. Girls in your position are born to be wives and mothers, to raise families that can continue building our financial wealth."

Mrs. Cassatt: "Raising children, caring for a husband, and running a household are a full-time job, Mary. How can you do that and have a career?"

Reading Le Figaro, 1878
Mary Cassatt, The Bridgeman Art Library/Getty Images

Mary:	"Well, maybe I don't want to raise children and care for a husband."
Mr. Cassatt:	"Preposterous. Do you expect me to support you all your life? How will you live without a husband?"
Mary:	"That's just my point. I want to support myself."
Mr. Cassatt:	"Doing what?"
Mary:	"Painting. I want to be an artist."
Mrs. Cassatt:	"But, Mary. Women paint for… enjoyment. For relaxation. To develop an eye for color that they can use in decorating their homes. Women don't paint for a living."
Mary:	"I will."
Mr. Cassatt:	"Impossible! Artists are bohemians. They never know where next week's rent is coming from. They live on hand-outs from family and friends. And their lifestyle is…not at all like what you are used to, Mary. Not at all like the lifestyle of most decent people."
Mary:	"Father, you are being unfair."
Mr. Cassatt:	"And besides." The art world is all male. All of the artists are men. All of the dealers

	are men. All of the buyers are men. How can you expect to earn two dollars in a business dominated by men?"
Mary:	"That's changing. And I intend to help speed that change. I will be a successful artist."
Mr. Cassatt:	"I'd almost rather see you dead."

Those were very strong words from a father who dearly loved his daughter. But those words tell how opposed Mr. Cassatt was to Mary's thought of becoming an artist.

But Mary was determined. And as long as she had gotten this far in this difficult conversation, Mary decided to unveil another surprise.

"The best place for me to learn to be an artist is in Europe," she said. "That's where all of the great works of art are. That's where I must learn to paint."

Mary was 16 at the time. She was proposing to choose a career instead of marriage; to support herself on the measly earnings of a painter; and to prepare herself by leaving home and living on her own in a foreign country, an ocean away from her family.

Mr. Cassatt saw that his daughter was serious. Rather than simply "put his foot down," he came up with a different suggestion. The United States was on the verge of a Civil War. It was not a good time to be traveling anywhere.

"Suppose you attend art school here in Philadelphia," he suggested. "The Pennsylvania Academy of Fine Art here is known as one of the best in the country. After you finish the program here, if you still want to study in Europe, we will talk about it then." He was probably thinking that by the end of the four-year course of study at the Academy, Mary will have gotten over this "crazy" idea of wanting to become an artist.[6]

Mary did not want to upset her parents further, so she accepted the compromise.

Mary Attends the Academy of Fine Art

Mary began her studies at The Pennsylvania Academy of Fine Art. The term "fine arts" refers to the arts concerned with the beautiful rather than the practical. Painting and sculpture are fine arts. The only reason for a painting or piece of sculpture is to have people look at it and enjoy it. On the other hand, carpentry might be considered a practical art. That is, a carpenter builds something that is useful, like a table. It may be a beautiful table but its practical function is the main reason for building it.

The Pennsylvania Academy was one of the first art schools in the country to admit women students. Classes for women, however, were separate from those for men. Women had other restrictions, too. They had to wear regular street clothes at all times. They could not wear special clothes just for painting. At the time, women's street clothes meant floor-length skirts and blouses with puffy sleeves. Not only did these clothes make painting cumbersome. But paint would frequently drip on them.[7]

One program feature that Mary liked was learning by copying. That is, the students spent much time studying works of established artists and trying to imitate those works. By trying to duplicate a painting, an art student

Pennsylvania Academy Modeling Class, 1862
Gihon and Rixon photographers
Courtesy of the Pennsylvania Academy of Fine Arts Archives

learns much about the craft. For instance, by copying from pictures, Mary learned the proportions of the human body and the structure of the face. That is so important when trying to capture the human face or body in a painting.

Mary and the other students went to the Philadelphia Museum of Art to copy master works of some great Italian, Dutch, and French painters.[8]

Mary was a serious art student but she also was a very sociable young woman. At the Academy, Mary formed friendships with many students—male and female. Some of these remained her close friends for many years.

The Academy was different from the typical school. For instance, most classes were held without a teacher. The students were told what they had to do, but worked on their own. Sometimes advanced students gave comments to younger students about their work. But there was no teacher to instruct students on how to paint. For that instruction, students had to seek out teachers outside of the school.[9]

The Rules of Art

The Academy insisted that students follow the "rules of art." One rule had to do with subjects of the paintings. The rule said that only certain subjects were fit for painting. Important historical events were suitable subjects. So were scenes from Greek and Roman mythology. Still life (fruit and flowers), portraits, and landscapes were also acceptable. Students had to limit themselves to painting these types of subjects. If someone wanted to paint a sailboat on a lake, she would be told: "That's not a suitable subject. It is not within the rules."

The rules were also specific about each painting's size. The size of the painting had to match the subject. That is, still life had to be in small paintings. Portraits had to be life size. Large paintings were reserved for the historical and mythological subjects.

In addition, the rules dictated how the elements in a painting were to be laid out. Larger figures were to be in the center of the painting. Smaller figures had to be placed at the edges. Backgrounds were to be done in darker colors; lighter colors would highlight the figures. Bright colors— red, yellow, green—could be used only in small areas.

The purpose of a painting, according to the rules, was to inspire fine feelings in the viewer. It should raise the viewer above the ordinary happenings of everyday life. Painting was not the place for an artist to comment on a social problem. For example, a painting was not the place for showing the tragedy of homelessness. Such a painting would disturb the viewer. The rules said paintings should not disturb; they should inspire "fine feelings."

Another rule dealt with the artist's feelings. The rule said those feelings had to be held out of the painting. The artist had to paint "what is there." The artist could not inject anything into the painting to convey her joy or sadness. In that sense, the painting had to be more like a photograph. Though the artist might have felt strongly about a subject, those emotions had to be held in check.

Rules, of course, help students learn the basics. But sometimes rules can stifle a person's creativity. Students at the Academy had to follow the rules very closely. They were not allowed to experiment. They could not go outside the barriers of the rules.

Mary had a hard time abiding by all of these rules. Yet she—as all of the students—was judged on how well her work reflected the rules. Anyone who did not paint according to the rules would have a hard time succeeding as an artist at the Academy.

Despite her attitude toward "the rules," Mary completed the four-year course at the Academy successfully. But she was not happy. She wanted to paint in her own way. She became bored painting according to the rules. She felt she was not learning anything new. She was not growing as an artist. While the Philadelphia Museum had some great works of art, it did not have many that she could learn from. She knew she had much more to learn about painting. "But I'm not learning it here," she probably said. "The place to learn is Europe."[10]

2

On Her Own in Europe

Mary completed her studies at the Academy, as she said she would. Her father hoped that by this time Mary would have given up the idea of becoming an artist. She hadn't. She was more determined than ever to be a painter. And to be the kind of painter she wanted to be, she would have to go to Europe.

This time, her father was more agreeable to her plans. He realized she was committed to her goals. She had gone along with his suggestion that she study in Philadelphia for four years. She was now 20 years old. The Civil War in the United States was ending. So, reluctantly, he gave his permission for Mary to move to France to study art. He even gave her an allowance to help pay her expenses.

Though she was fearless, Mary didn't go to France alone. Eliza Haldeman, a friend and art student at the Academy, went with her. Eliza, too, wanted a career in art. Mrs. Cassatt also traveled with the two young women, to help them get settled in their new "home."

Mary in Paris

The Paris that Mary and Eliza moved to in 1865 was the center of the art world. In fact, the city itself was very much a work of art. In the latter half of the 19th century, Emperor Napoleon III had the city renovated and rebuilt. Many streets and the transportation system were totally redone. The train stations, for instance, were given vaulted ceilings and glass roofs. Paris had become a model for cities throughout the world.[11]

The number one art school in Paris was the Ecole des Beaux Arts–the School of Fine Art. But the school did not accept women students. So Mary became a private student of Jean Leon Geromme, one of the best painters and teachers in Paris. Mary also studied at the atelier, or studio, of a popular painter named Charles Chaplain. But she didn't work with him for very long. His teaching was just more concentration on the same old rules she had learned at the Academy in Philadelphia.[12] She hadn't gone to Paris for that.

But in Paris Mary enjoyed the opportunity to copy paintings that hung in the Louvre Museum. This huge old palace was–and is today–one of the most famous museums in the world. The Louvre is home to the world's largest collection of painting and sculpture. Mary had what she wanted–the chance to study and learn from so many of the great masterpieces.

Mary worked hard. But she also had fun. In addition to Eliza Haldeman, Mary had other friends in Paris, some from the United States. Eliza wrote in a letter to her family: "There is a quantity of our old artist acquaintances over here (Paris) just now and I am afraid the Louvre will become a second Academy for talking and amusing ourselves." [13]

Mary Tours the Countryside

Having had the "city experience," Mary and her friend Eliza wanted to see what life was like elsewhere. After living in Paris for some time, they moved to a small village–E'couen. Here they saw a totally different France. Instead of crowded city streets, they saw rolling fields and hills. They saw farmers and shepherds. Instead of men and women dressed in the latest fashions, they saw peasant people very plainly dressed and living very simple lives. Mary and Eliza now had many new subjects for their paintings.

The young artists then traveled to the coast of Normandy. They climbed the hills of Provence and the mountains of Savoy. They saw in person the spectacular Mediterranean Sea and Mont Blanc. After months of soaking in a "different" France, the two artists returned to Paris with "notebooks full of sketches" they were eager to put to canvas. [14]

These travels were typical for American students in Europe. Another of Mary's friends, Emily Sartain, wrote in a letter to her father: "Do you think I ought to go (to Rome) or not? I am going to Paris in May, on my way will stop at Milan (Italy)–and perhaps go to Venice (Italy)–what do you think?" [15]

At a time when women–especially in the United States–had little freedom, these young artists were crisscrossing Europe. Most of the women they had grown up with were back in the United States living very ordinary lives. Mary and her friends, meanwhile, were getting to know places, people, and cultures that were so different.

Mary Confronts the Salon

All of her travels and work brought Mary to a point where she wanted to sell her work. The route to almost all sales took an artist through "the Salon." "The Salon" was the name given to an art competition sponsored by the French government. Each year the government invited artists to submit paintings. Judges selected about 1000 of "the best" to hang in the huge hall. ("Salon" is the French word for "hall.")People then came to view the paintings and buy those they liked. So, if painters wanted to sell

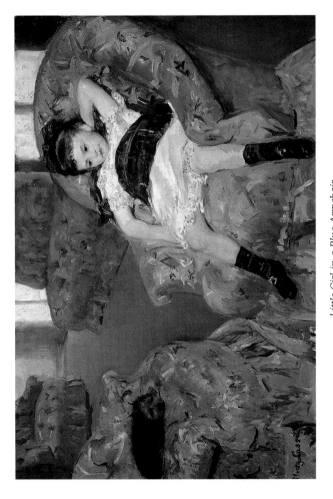

Little Girl in a Blue Armchair
1983.1.18:(2893)/PA: Cassatt, Mary
Little Girl in a Blue Armchair, Collection of Mr. and Mrs. Paul Mellon, Image © 2004 Board of Trustees, National Gallery of Art, Washington,1878, oil on canvas, (35 1/2 x 29 1/4)

paintings, their work would first have to be accepted by the Salon judges.

The judges had very strict ideas of what was good art. Just as at the Academy, a short set of rules dictated what and how artists must paint. The Salon encouraged artists to be very conventional. That is, they should paint as artists have always painted. They should not do anything different or unusual. The subjects should be traditional subjects, such as still life, landscapes, portraits, and historical and mythological events. The paintings should be perfectly finished, having very smooth brushstrokes. [16]

During her second year in France, Mary submitted work to the Salon–without success. She submitted a number of paintings that were rejected. Finally the Salon jury selected one of Mary's paintings. The painting was titled "The Mandolin Player."

But one acceptance didn't mean she was a success. The Salon rejected numerous others. One of her paintings, of a woman knitting, was rejected because the background was too light. The rules called for dark backgrounds because paintings were supposed to be serious. After Mary darkened the background, the painting was accepted. [17]

In a letter to a friend, Mary expressed her displeasure with the judge and jury system: "the jury consisted of three people, one of which was a pharmacist." [18] Her point was that a handful of judges had total control of the paintings that the public could see and that artists could sell. Many of these judges, she claimed, were not art experts. They were not qualified to make such decisions. Yet these judges seemed to hold Mary's future in their hands.

3

Opportunity Knocks

After almost five years in France, Mary still had achieved little success. She was trying to paint for the judges at the Salon and at the same time to paint in her own style. She had seen the works of some artists who defied the judges' rules and she liked those paintings. But these artists were not selling many of their paintings. So she was still torn between painting to please the judges and painting to please herself.

Disappointed But Not Defeated

Suddenly, things changed. In 1870, Prussia, a German state, attacked France. This conflict became known as the

Franco-Prussian War. Paris was no longer safe. Nor was much of the surrounding area. So Mary had to return to the United States.[19]

Once home, Mary set up a studio in Philadelphia, as some of her friends had done. She resumed her painting. She made every effort to sell her work. She took paintings to galleries in New York but didn't sell any. She then went to Chicago. Not only did she not sell any paintings there, but her paintings were destroyed in a fire.[20] After many years of study and hard work, Mary was discouraged. "Will I ever be able to make a living through my painting?" she may have wondered.

Mary felt restricted by the "rules" mentality. It was even stronger in the United States than in Europe. And the collections of art she could view in the U.S. were very small compared to those in Europe. To make matters worse, her family moved to a small town called Hollidaysburg. Mary had to give up her studio in Philadelphia. She found this small town even more confining. She wrote to her friend Emily Sartain: "I have given up my studio ... and have not touched a brush for six weeks, nor ever will again until I see some prospect of getting back to Europe." [21]

Though Mary had lived in France, she had not spent much time in Spain. She had learned enough about Spanish painting, though, to realize she must see those great works in person. In another letter to Emily, Mary wrote:

> "Alas! We don't seem any nearer (to Spain) than we were some months ago, at least I don't. I have been abandoning

myself to despair and homesickness, for I really feel as if it was intended I should be a Spaniard and quite a mistake that I was born in America." [22]

But Mary did not give up. As often happens when people continue to work toward their goals, Mary's fortunes turned. An opportunity arose unexpectedly. A bishop in Pittsburgh had seen some of Mary's work and liked it. He thought her style was suited to some paintings he wanted done. He liked two religious paintings done many years before by an Italian artist named Corregio. The bishop wanted someone to copy those paintings so he could hang them in the cathedral in Pittsburgh. He asked Mary if she would like to paint those copies. The bishop told her the originals were in Parma, Italy, and she would have to go there to see them. Mary, of course, accepted immediately.[23]

Here was a dream come true. She received this assignment, for which she would be paid. She would be going to Europe to do it. And the bishop would pay her travel expenses.

So in 1871, at age 27, Mary was once again on an ocean liner. She and her friend Emily Sartain were sailing to Italy and to the next phase in Mary's career.

Mary in Italy

Mary studied the works of Corregio in the domed cathedral in Parma. While studying the Corregio paintings, as well as others, Mary was drawing sketches of many different kinds of figures, such as happy, frolicking angels. She sketched images of humans at every angle. She studied Corregio's technique. She saw how he used shading to make figures look rounded and three-dimensional. She saw how he put light on faces to create a more dramatic look. [24]

She also studied religious works of other painters in Parma and in other cities throughout Italy. Though those paintings were religious in nature, Mary found them to be worldly and realistic in style.[25] The subject of many of these religious paintings was the Madonna and Child. This subject may have had a powerful impact on Mary. Some years later she painted many pictures of mothers and their children.

Parma, Italy, was not crowded with American artists and tourists, as Paris was. Mary and Emily mixed in well in the Italian artistic and social circles. They got to know art teachers as well as artists themselves. Many were eager to help the two American artists. [26] Mary knew from experience that the classroom is not the only place for learning. We can learn some of our most important lessons in conversations with different people.

While in Italy, Mary developed a pattern of work that served her well for many years. She began a painting with a simple drawing in pencil or charcoal. She used pencil or charcoal so she could easily erase and change the drawing as she went along. She might have made a dozen or more sketches before settling on the right one for the painting. Next, she worked out the difficult parts of the painting.

Those parts might deal with figures, background, details–anything that might prove troublesome. Then she would do the drawing on canvas. She would choose her colors, mixing the oils to get just the right shades. Only then would she bring in the model to pose. By that time Mary knew exactly the pose she would want the model to take. She would then spend weeks–sometimes months–working on a single painting.[27] The bishop liked the copies Mary made of the Corregio paintings.

Mary in Spain

The following year Mary moved to Spain. She lived in Madrid for six months. She studied the great masterpieces in the Prado, another famous museum. From Madrid, Mary went to Seville, where she lived for five months. From the works of Spanish painters Velazquez, Moya, and Murillo, Mary learned to use heavier dollops of paint. You may recall that the rules in the Academy insisted that brushstrokes had to be very smooth and

Mary Cassatt ca. 1872
Baroni and Gardelli photographers
Courtesy The Pennsylvania
Academy of Fine Arts Archives

finished. Mary felt that using heavier dollops of paint gave more texture to the pictures. The texture created the feeling that the viewer could walk into the scene. [28]

In a letter to her friend Emily, Mary raved about the paintings she was seeing in Spain. "Velazquez. Oh my, but you know how to paint....The men and women (in the Velazquez paintings) have a reality about them which exceeds anything I ever supposed possible. Velazquez's (painting) 'Spinners', good heavens, why you can walk into the picture." [29] Mary then added: "Emily, do do come (to Spain). You will never regret it."

On her own, Mary was free to paint what she wanted, as she wanted. She did not have to conform to any rule or follow the dictates of teachers. She was painting what she was seeing. In Spain, bullfighting was very popular. So Mary painted bullfighters (called "toreadors") into her canvases. In 1873, she submitted her painting "Offering the Panale to the Toreador" to the Salon. It was accepted.[30]

The painting reflects much of the style she saw in Spanish masterpieces. Mary placed brightly lit figures against dark backgrounds to make the people stand out. [31] Mary also limited the background details, to have viewers focus on the conversation taking place between the two subjects. [32]

The Salon also accepted Mary's "On the Balcony." This painting, too, shows the influence of the paintings Mary had seen in Spain.

Offering the Panale to the Bullfighter –
Sterling and Francine Clark Art Institute, Williamston, Massachusetts

We can see that, over time, the Salon was more willing to accept Mary's breaks from tradition. Her "Woman Reading in the Garden" is a good example. In some ways, the painting meets the traditional conventions. The figure is in the center and the background colors are dark. But one can see signs of Mary's style changing. The subject is not conventional. The ordinary activity of a woman reading a newspaper is not a conventional subject. Yet the Salon accepted the painting. [33]

Mary was slowly gaining confidence. She was moving away from the rules. She was finding her own style. The time she spent in Spain had influenced that style. She learned much in Spain. But now she was ready to return to the center of the art world. She headed back to Paris.

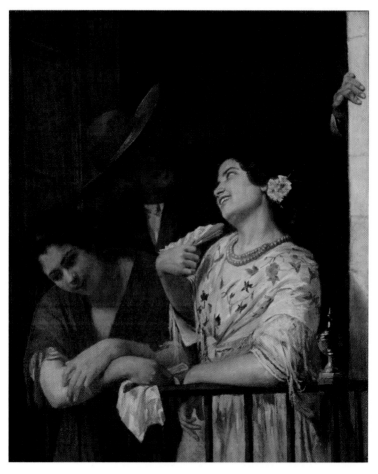

On the Balcony
W1906-1-7 Cassatt, Mary Stevenson
Philadelphia Museum of Art: Gift of John G. Johnson
for the W.P. Wilstach Collection, 1906

Woman Reading in the Garden,
Mary Cassatt, © *Frances G. Mayer/Corbis*

4

Breaking the Rules

Back in Paris, Mary continued to work. One day she had an experience that changed her life.

Walking past a gallery in Paris, Mary spotted a painting in the window. It shows a group of dancers at a ballet class. The dancers are taking instruction from the dance master. Mary stared at it for a long time. She came back to look at it often. "I used to go and flatten my nose against the window and absorb all I could of his (the painter's) art. It changed my life. I saw art as I wanted to see it. I began to live." [34]

Mary and the "Independents"

The painting that captured Mary's heart was "Ballet Rehearsal" by Edgar Degas. It was done in pastel, a kind of chalklike crayon used in drawing. Usually pastels are in soft, pale colors. The painting has lines that make the dancers and the master seem to move. The figures are at unusual angles and in informal poses. [35] This scene was simple and from everyday life. In addition, viewers could sense the feelings of the painter. All of these features broke the rules of the Academy and the Salon.

At the time–1874–Degas was an established artist. Many of his paintings had been accepted by the Salon. But he was not happy with the jury system of the Salon. Like Mary, he wanted to paint his own way.

So Degas founded a group of artists who thought as he did. They called themselves the "Independents," because they did not want to be governed by the rules of the Salon. The members worked on their own. They had their own styles. They met often to discuss art and ways of getting their work displayed.

Degas and the Independents planned their own exhibit. They called their exhibit the Salon des Refuses (Hall of the Rejected). [36] They gave their exhibit that name because most of their work had been rejected by the Salon judges.

Critics who attended the exhibit said: "These people can't paint. All they do is give their impressions of what they see." From that point on, these independent-thinking artists have been called "Impressionists."

How the Impressionists were Different

The Impressionists chose subjects from everyday settings–gardeners, maids, farmers at work. Dancers performing or rehearsing. Mothers tending to their children.

The Impressionists used bright colors; they avoided dark colors and shadows. They went outside the studio to work so they could bring into their paintings the changing effects of the winds, the clouds, and the sunlight. [37]

According to the "rules," a painting should represent "what is." It should be as close to the original subject as possible, like a photograph. The Impressionists did not paint that way. They wanted to leave exact likenesses to the photographers. Painters, they said, should not seek to create an exact likeness to a person or object. [38] The Impressionists tried instead to convey a feeling and a mood that are part of a scene. Traditional artists would sketch a scene and then go back to the studio to paint it. Impressionists would do the painting right there on the spot. In that way they could capture the light and the mood at the moment. They could also capture their feelings. [39]

The Impressionists had a different way of filling in space on a canvas. They used hundreds of brushstrokes and dabs. Their strokes might be straight, curved, thick, thin, broken, smooth, dotted, blurry, squiggly, or zigzag.[40] These artists used whatever conveyed the proper impression.

The Impressionists shared the desire to make the modern world the subject for art. But each one went about it differently. Monet, for instance, focused on outdoor life. Degas painted everyday indoor scenes.[41] Cezanne captured scenes of city crowds and public theaters. What they had in common was the desire to break the hold of the "rules."

The Salon judges, of course, did not like this break from tradition. They thought the subjects the Impressionists painted were "vulgar," because they were of ordinary people and scenes. They didn't like the Impressionists' use of light colors. They thought the drawing was sloppy. They thought Impressionists' use of very visible brushstrokes was another definite no-no. [42]

The Impressionists were ridiculed at first. But the group attracted a number of artists who eventually became recognized among the greatest artists of all time. Among these are Manet, Cezanne, Monet, Pissarro, Renoir, and the founder, Degas.

Mary Makes a Choice

Some time before the first Hall of the Rejected exhibit, Mary had a painting accepted at the Salon. She called it "Ida." Degas happened to see it, and liked it. "Here is someone who feels as I do," he said about the painter whom he did not yet know.

He invited Mary to join the Impressionists' group. She was thrilled. But she first had to think about it. There were reasons not to accept that invitation. If she joined the Impressionists, she knew the Salon judges would scorn her work. People who thought the way the judges did would not buy her paintings.

But Mary saw reasons why she should join the Impressionist group. The most important reason was that painting to please judges worked against her ideas of what an artist is. In pleasing the judges, she would be displeasing herself. So Mary chose the independent Impressionists over the Salon.

Instead of taking the safe route (with the Salon), Mary took a chance on herself. She followed her heart. Once she did, she said: "I took leave of conventional art. I began to live." [43]

In a letter, she wrote: "At last, I could work with absolute independence without considering the opinion of a jury." [44]

What Mary Learned from Degas

Mary became close friends with Degas. He was older and more experienced. So he could offer valuable comment on her work. From Degas, Mary learned to mix oils with turpentine, to make colors look richer and brighter. She gained confidence in painting pictures of everyday life. These included subjects such as people at the theater as well as in the home. [45]

Mary was not afraid of being around intelligent, forceful people like Degas. While she learned much from him, she did not slavishly imitate his work. She kept her own personal attitudes and beliefs about her art. She freely spoke her opinions to Degas. When she disagreed with him, she

Mary Cassatt, Seated, with Photographs by Edgar Degas, 1884
© Francis G. Mayer/CORBIS

told him so. He admired that spirit in her. [46]

Under Degas' influence, Mary altered her style somewhat. She began focusing more on people and using light colors.[47] "The Loge" shows that influence. Mary uses countless lines and squiggles in many colors to make up the women's dresses, skin, and hair. Also in the Degas-Impressionist style, the women are in an ordinary scene (the theater). They are in casual poses, as if paying no attention to the artist–as if they don't realize they are being painted. [48]

Success Comes Slowly

Mary was one of only three women who were invited to display their work at the Salon des Refuses. Eleven of Mary's paintings and drawings were displayed in the "Rejected" exhibit in 1879. Thousands of people came to the exhibit, but few bought anything. Mary earned 40 francs, which was about $100.00–not a lot of money for all of the work and time she had put in.

But Mary found encouraging words in some of the critics' reviews. One art critic compared her work to Degas's. Another wrote:

> "There is not a painting, nor a pastel by Mademoiselle Mary Cassatt that is not an exquisite symphony of color. Mary Cassatt is fond of pure colors and possesses the secret of blending them in a composition that is bold, mysterious, and fresh." [49]

Mary Remains Independent

From that point on, Mary's popularity began to grow. Though she shared the Impressionists' thinking, and much of their painting style, Mary didn't surrender her traditional training. So her works did not appear as radical or "strange" as the works of other Impressionists. As a result, more people in the mainstream of the art world liked her paintings. Though she was in the inner circle of the Impressionist movement, she was able to stay independent of the group. That is, she could paint the way she wanted, no matter who did or didn't like it.

Mary continued to display her work at the Hall of the Rejected exhibits. She sold a number of her paintings. Her reputation was spreading.

Mary Helps Other Artists and Art

Then the Impressionists did not have an exhibit for three years. So Mary stepped in to help the Impressionists in a number of ways. In 1886, Mary helped sponsor and organize another exhibit. Around the same time, she began having Impressionists' work shown in America. Mary was happy to find that people from her homeland liked her work and that of the other Impressionists. [50] Partly through the efforts of her brother Aleck, Mary's paintings and those of other Impressionists were catching on in America.

Aleck was then president of the Pennsylvania Railroad. He knew many people who loved and bought art. Aleck

The Loge by Mary Cassatt, ca. 1880
© Francis G. Mayer/CORBIS

Young woman working in the garden, c.1880-82
Mary Cassatt, The Bridgeman Art Library/Getty Images

introduced these people to Mary's work. He also showed them the paintings of other Impressionists. So, besides selling their paintings in Europe, many Impressionist painters were also selling their work in America.

In addition, Mary persuaded her brother to buy works of Manet, Monet, Morisot, Renoir, and Pissarro. In doing so, he became the first collector of Impressionist art in the United States.[51]

Mary also advised others to invest in Impressionist art. She convinced her friend Louisine Elder Havemeyer to use all of her spending money (about $100) to buy Degas' "Ballet Rehearsal." [52] Today that painting may be worth millions of dollars. That was the first painting Louisine ever bought. She and her husband, however, went on to create one of the finest private art collections in the world.

After more than 20 years of struggling, Mary had finally launched her career. Despite all of the obstacles, she was an artist, painting the kind of pictures she wanted to paint.

5

Mary Paints Woman's Progress

Though Mary lived in France, one of the most important events in her career took place in Chicago. That's where the World's Columbian Exposition was being held in 1892. At the Exposition, countries from around the world displayed their achievements in science, technology, manufacturing, and the arts. The Exposition enabled people to see the progress made in nations they might never visit.

The Chicago Exposition would include a "Woman's Building." An entire building would be devoted to the progress women had made over the years. A woman architect would design the building. Women would decorate it. And all of the inventions, designs, and artwork displayed would be created by women. [53]

The Exposition committee wanted to tell the story of women's progress through pictures. In that way, language would not be a barrier for anyone. So the committee decided to tell that story through murals. A mural is a large wall painting. Some murals are painted directly on the wall. In another type, the painter paints on canvas or another substance, which is then pasted right to the wall. There is no frame surrounding the mural.

Mary Paints "Modern Woman"

For the Exposition, the committee wanted one mural to show "Primitive Woman." That is, the painting would show women from many, many years earlier. The second mural would show "Modern Woman." By looking at the two murals, viewers would see women's growth and achievement over the centuries.

The committee asked Mary to paint the mural for "Modern Woman." At first, Mary was hesitant. She had never painted a mural before. Nor had she ever done a painting as large as the one she was asked to paint. The committee wanted a painting that was 58 feet long and 12 feet high. In a letter to her friend Louisine Elder

Havermeyer, Mary explained her thinking:

> I am going to do a decoration for the Chicago Exposition. When the committee offered it to me to do, at first I was horrified, but gradually began to think it would be great fun to do something I have never done before. And as the idea of such a thing put Degas in a rage and he did not spare every criticism he could think of, I got my spirit up and I said I would not give up the idea for anything. [54]

Mary's reasoning shows us much about the woman. First, she was a bit "horrified" at the thought of taking on an assignment that was totally new to her. Then she thought it might be "fun" to try something new. That willingness to accept a new challenge is a trait of successful people. Mary was then 48 years old but she still wanted to grow as an artist. She was still willing to try something different. Second, Degas told her not to do it. The sort of mural the committee wanted was not the kind of painting that he and the other Impressionists did. That made Mary even more interested in doing it. Her sense of independence came through again. One sure way of getting Mary interested in doing something was to tell her not to do it.

Mary worked on the mural at her studio in France. The size of the painting would be a problem. How would she be able to paint a canvas that was 12-feet tall? She did not want to stand on a ladder to paint. So she had workers dig a trench in her garden. A trench is long, narrow ditch. The trench was 60 feet long and six feet deep. When she had to work on the upper portion of the painting, she had it lowered into the trench. To work on the lower portion, she had it raised. [55]

Mary planned her mural in three panels, or sections. Each panel would show a different stage of womanhood.

The panel on the left showed adolescent, or teenage, girls chasing after a figure that symbolizes Fame. Young women, Mary is saying, have many dreams, hopes, and ambitions. Geese are chasing after the young women, honking at them. These geese represent people who try to keep young women from pursuing their dreams. (Mary may have had her father in mind, as he had tried to keep her from her career in art.)

In the murals' center panel, more mature, educated women are plucking fruit from a tree. This image represents women seeking knowledge. They are also sharing that knowledge. The women are working together. One stands atop a ladder handing fruit down to another. Two women carry a bushel of fruit together. It's important to remember that when Mary lived, very few women went beyond eighth grade in school. Only boys and men went further, especially into technical and scientific learning.

In the panel on the right, one woman plays a banjo. Another woman dances, while a third enjoys the music and dancing. This panel suggests the contributions women have made to art. It also indicates women's role in appreciating and spreading culture.

Mary said of the mural: "I have tried to make the general effect as bright, as gay, as amusing as possible. The occasion is one of rejoicing, a great national fete." [56]

Modern Woman, by Mary Cassatt, decoration of south tympanum, Woman's building; Worlds Columbian Exposition; Chicago (Ill); 1893: Credit: Chicago Historical Society

Mary, the Genteel Rebel

The subject of this mural was very close and important to Mary. Throughout her life, Mary had to struggle to overcome barriers placed before women. First, her family challenged her desire to have a career and become a painter. Then some of the art schools she attended did not fully support training for women. When she continued to pursue her dream, many in the art world were still reluctant to take a woman artist seriously. Even among the "independent-thinking" Impressionists, Mary was the first of only a few women to be accepted.

Against this opposition, Mary waged a quiet revolution. One might call her a "genteel rebel." She did not march in protest against unfairness. Instead, she went quietly about her career. She let her determination and her work prove to people that women could be just as creative and successful as men could be. The mural gave Mary the chance to speak out even more boldly for the rights of women. In a letter to Bertha Palmer, a member of the Exposition committee, Mary made it clear that she was hoping the mural would send a message about the place of women in the world:

> An American friend asked me in a rather huffy tone the other day, "Then this is woman apart from her relations to man?" I told him it was. Men, I have no doubt, are painted in all their vigor on the walls of the other buildings (in the Exposition); to us (women), the sweetness of childhood, the charm of womanhood, if I have not conveyed some sense of that charm, in one word if I have not been absolutely feminine, then I have failed." [57]

Not everyone liked the mural. Some did not understand the symbolism behind the images. That is, they did not understand that the honking geese were critics of young women with dreams and ambitions. They didn't understand that the image of women picking fruit referred to women's seeking knowledge. Others didn't like Mary's use of strong colors in the mural. In addition, many viewers at the Exposition had a hard time seeing the figures in the painting. The largest of the figures were just smaller than life-size. But the mural was hung in a huge hall some 40 feet above the floor. That explains why some could not clearly make out the figures. [58]

Many, however, liked the mural very much. Bertha Palmer of the Exposition committee, wrote to Mary: "I consider your panels by far the most beautiful thing that has been done for the Exposition....It (the mural) is so simple, strong, and sincere, so modern and yet so primitive." [59]

Strangely, the huge mural disappeared. At the close of the Exposition, the mural was taken down and put in storage. No one ever saw it again.

But the experience had a great impact on Mary's career. The mural placed Mary in the forefront of the movement for a woman's right to be whoever she wanted to be.[60]

A number of paintings grew out of the work she had done on the mural. For example, "Baby Reaching for an Apple" (1893) suggests that knowledge and science are within the reach of every child. The older woman in the

Child Picking a Fruit –
Virginia Museum of Fine Arts, Richmond. Gift of Ivor and Anne Massey.
Photo: Wen Hwa Ts'ao. © Virginia Museum of Fine Arts.

painting, however, is helping the next generation to gain that knowledge.[61] This painting combines Mary's "mother-and-child" theme with the theme of women advancing in the world.

Mary committed herself to paintings that showed in different ways the significant roles women play in the world.

6

Mary Works for the Right to Vote

Mary Cassatt was not the typical woman of the late 19th and early 20th centuries. She was educated. She traveled freely. She lived on her own. She had a career. But she was typical of the "New Woman" that was emerging. These women wanted to see more opportunities for women. They wanted the chance to be doctors, lawyers, writers, artists, thinkers, and social workers.[62] They did not think it was fair–or good for society–if women did not have the same opportunities that men had.

Women Need the Right to Vote

One important piece in changing the attitudes of society would be for women to vote. Today American women have the right to vote and hold political office. That was not the case in Mary's day. Only men could vote. Mary felt this was an injustice.

Most of her life she waged a battle against injustice on her own. She did not participate in the organized movements for women's rights. But as she grew older, she saw that women would not be accepted as equals unless they could vote. So she joined with others in campaigning for what was called "Women's Suffrage"–the right to vote.

Interest in women's rights was not new. It began as early as 1848–more than 50 years prior to Mary's joining the fight. That's when the First Congress for American Women's Rights was held in Seneca Falls, New York. Since then, women made some progress, but slowly. Some extended their education. Some even went to college. Some trained to be doctors. Some traveled. But 50 years after that first Congress was held, no American woman enjoyed the right to vote.[63]

Mary and World War I

Mary believed that women were thoughtful of people's welfare. Because of that, women would use the vote to improve the world situation. [64] One situation that needed improving was the war going on in Europe at the time. People said it would be "the war to end all wars." But it

Mary Cassatt at Villa Angelotto Grasse, 1913 (#6)
Archives, Hill-Stead Museum, Farmington, CT

wasn't, as a number of wars followed. So this war was named World War I. It was called a "world" war because many countries fought in it. These included France, Germany, England, and the United States.

Mary was living outside of Paris at the time. She had to leave her home for fear of being hurt in an air raid. Mary wrote about the war in a letter to her friend Louisine Elder Havemeyer: "The great drama is opening around us! How will it all end? ...Work for suffrage, for it is the women who will decide the question of life or death for a nation." [65]

In a letter to another friend, Mary picked up the same theme, but in even stronger terms: "If the women of Germany were more on an equal (basis) with the men, the atrocities of this war would have been avoided." [66]

How Mary Helps Win the Vote

Getting a new law enacted takes a lot of persuading. It requires many people because there is much to do. These "activists" have to write, publish, and distribute pamphlets explaining the argument–in this case for women's suffrage. People have to give speeches in front of many groups. They have to get in front of Congressmen (at that time everyone in Congress was a man). Congress would ultimately make the decision to pass a new law granting women the vote. All of this effort requires money.

To raise money for this campaign, Mary's friend, Louisine Elder Havemeyer, arranged for a benefit art exhibit in New York. It was called the "Suffrage Loan

Exhibition of Old Masters and Works by Edgar Degas and Mary Cassatt."[67] Mary gladly had some of her paintings displayed at the exhibit. She persuaded Degas and other artist friends to do the same.

One of Degas's paintings was owned by a man named Colonel Paine. Mary thought this painting had to be in the New York exhibit. So she wrote to the Colonel asking him to lend the painting to the exhibit. In her letter, she combined two of her major interests–art and suffrage:

> I ... appeal to you as a patriotic American to lend your Degas (painting) to the exhibition Mrs. Havemeyer is arranging. The sight of that picture may be the turning point in the life of some young American painter. The first sight of Degas' pictures was the turning point in my artistic life.
>
> Never mind the object of the exhibition. Think only of the young painters. As to the suffrage for women, it must come as a result of this awful war. With the slaughter of millions of men, women will be forced, are now being forced, to do their work. And we have only begun. [68]

Mary encouraged her family and friends to attend the exhibit and support the cause for women's suffrage. But many people were opposed to the movement and would not attend. Even Mary's sister-in-law (Aleck's wife) and her children refused to attend. They were clinging to the idea that women had no business voting for the President, Congress, Governor, or any other political office. Mary became so annoyed that she gave away paintings she had been saving for her nieces and nephews. [69]

World War I began in 1914 and ended in 1918. Historians estimate that 10 million people died in the war. Another 20 million were wounded.

In 1919, the U.S. Congress passed the amendment to the constitution granting women the right to vote. In 1920, enough states ratified the amendment. That made it law–American women now had the right to vote. Mary was then 76 years old. Even at that age Mary had the spunk she had shown as a teenager.

7

Daughter, Sister, Aunt, and Friend

While Mary was building her career, she also had a personal life. That life centered around her family and friends.

Once Mary's parents got used to the idea of her having a career as an artist, they were very supportive. In fact, the entire family helped her in every way they could. So when Mary's sister Lydia became ill with a kidney disease, and her parents were aging, Mary gladly had them come to live with her. She not only cared for their health. But she also brought them into her work. The models in many of her paintings are family members.

Mary and Her Family

"Katherine Cassatt Reading to Her Grandchildren" is one of those paintings. In summer of 1880, two of Mary's nieces and a nephew came to France to spend the summer with their two aunts and grandparents. During that summer, Mary captured on canvas a scene that was repeated often–Grandmother Cassatt reading to her grandchildren.

After the children returned to the United States, Mrs. Cassatt wrote a letter to her granddaughter Katherine. In it, she wrote:

> "Do you remember the one (painting) she (Mary) painted of you and Rob and Elsie listening to me reading fairy tales? She finished it after you left and it is now at the exhibition. A gentleman wants to buy it but I don't think your Aunt Mary will sell it. She could hardly sell her mother and her nieces and nephew, I think."[70]

This painting reflects the closeness of the Cassatt family. The many paintings she did of family members and scenes in the home and garden show her deep inter-est in family. Though separated by an ocean, they all kept close contact through letters. In a letter that Mary wrote around Christmas time to one of her nephews, we see her love for him and all of her nieces and nephews. She writes about packaging Christmas gifts to be sent to the

Katherine Cassatt Reading to Her Grandchildren
Mary Cassatt, The Bridgeman Art Library/Getty Images

children. She also writes about painting, reading, and other things:

> While the Christmas box was being filled, we were con-
> stantly talking about you all, and trying to think of what you
> would all like best; I suppose you will have received the box
> before you get this (letter) and know if we guessed right.

> I want you to tell Rob from me that when he gets his
> paint box he must promise to draw very carefully a portrait of
> one of you, beginning with the eyes (remember) and send it
> to Grandmother; that would please her more than any other
> Christmas present she could get.

> Grandfather has been sending you some books; he hopes
> you will read them with care; when you write you can tell
> him if you have done so.

> We all send lots of love and kisses to you all. And we
> want you to write sometimes and not to forget your relations
> over here, for they think of you constantly. [71]

Mary encouraged her nieces and nephews to draw, paint, and read. She also wanted them to learn to ride horses. Mary rode since she was a little girl. When the children came to spend time with her, she often took them horseback riding. Mary herself continued to ride as an older woman, even after she broke her leg in a fall.

Family Sadness and Helpful Friends

Being so close to her family, Mary was very sad when tragedy struck. In 1882, Lydia died from a kidney disease. She had suffered a long time. Mary and the doctors gave her the best care possible. After Lydia's death, Mary was so upset she could not work for six months. [72]

Mary's mother's health was weakening. During the cold months, Mary took her to live in the south, where it was warmer. In 1891, nine years after Lydia's death, Mary's father died. Four years later, Mary's mother died.

During these very sad times, Mary's friends comforted her. Sometimes just sharing her feelings with friends–even in a letter–helped her through the worst days. She wrote to one friend: "The depression is at times very great. In fact, life seems very dark to me just now."[73]

Since she was a young girl, Mary attracted as friends many intelligent, achieving women. She often inspired them to lift their sights and try for better things. One of her friends, Emily Sartain, wrote about Mary's impact on her in a letter to her (Emily's) father: "Oh how good it is to be with someone (Mary) who talks understandably about Art. I find I soon get tired of even friends who are not interested cordially in painting."

In the same letter, Miss Sartain goes on to talk about how critical Mary could be. She also explains why that is:

> I by no means agree with all of Miss Cassatt's judgments. She is entirely too slashing...disdains the Salon pictures...we are used to revering–but her intolerance comes from the earnestness with which she loves nature and her profession–so I can sympathize with her.[74]

Despite the fact that they disagreed often, Mary and Emily remained close friends for many years. So did Eliza Haldeman and Louisine Elder Havemeyer, among others.

Mary also had a number of male friends. Some of

Self-Portrait by Mary Cassatt The Metropolitan Museum of Art,
Bequest of Edith H. Proskauer, 1975.
(1975.319.1) Photograph © 1998 The Metropolitan Museum of Art.

these were artists, teachers, collectors, and gallery opera-tors. She also considered her brothers to be among her closest friends. [75]

Ever Independent

Mary, however, did not see the need to marry. It was not unusual for artistic women to marry late in life, or not at all. And Mary had her parents and her sister living with her, so she may not have felt the need for further companionship.[76] In addition, being single did not bother Mary. "I am independent," she wrote. "I can live alone and I love to work." [77] Her "Self-Portrait" shows us a woman who is completely at ease, confident in her painting and in herself."[78]

Serving Art in Different Ways

During those years and after, Mary did some of her best work. She had her paintings displayed in numerous exhibits. Among these was an exhibit in the United States in which only Mary's paintings were shown. It was during these years that she painted the massive mural for the Chicago Exposition and the numerous paintings that flowed from that mural.

She was named Chevalier of the Legion d'Honneur. The French government gave this award to people who made outstanding contributions to society. Rarely was this award ever given to a women or to an American.

Portrait of Mary Cassatt, ca. 1914.
Research material on Mary Cassatt and James A. McNeill Whistler, 1872-1975,
Archives of American Art, Smithsonian Institution.

Mary also became advisor to a number of art collectors. She would often travel with people like her friend, Louisine Elder Havemeyer, and help them pick out high quality works of art. Mrs. Havemeyer wrote of the help Mary had given her:

> I owe it to Miss Cassatt that I was able to see the Courbets (paintings). She ...explained Courbet to me, spoke of the great painter in her flowing, generous way, called my attention to his marvelous execution, to his color, above all to his realism....I listened to her with such attention as we stood before his pictures and I never forgot it. [79]

Mary's health was failing. She was diagnosed with diabetes. Then her eyesight began to weaken. For the last 15 years of her life, failing eyesight kept Mary from painting. [80] In time, she became totally blind. On June 14, 1926, Mary died at the age of 82.

Gaining Self-Confidence from Mary Cassatt

If there is one thing you can learn from Mary Cassatt, it is the importance of self-confidence. Though more opportunities exist for girls today than they did in Mary's time, girls and women still face resistance.

Thinking of Mary can help you to overcome that resistance. Mary would not be denied. She would not let others put her down or stand in her way. She accomplished all she did largely because she believed in herself. You can do the same.

A Career
on Canvas

Mary Cassatt chose to be an artist who followed her own heart. As we look at her paintings we see clear reflections of the person and artist that she was at different times of her life.

"A Mandolin Player" (1868) was the first of Mary's paintings that the judges at the Salon accepted. She was still unsure of herself at this point early in her career. So she signed the painting "Mary Stevenson" (her middle name). The painting shows that Mary was following most of the rules of painting she had learned at the Pennsylvania Academy. The figure is in the center of the painting, as the rules said it should be. The background is in dark colors. Yet there is a bit of the unconventional in the subject. A woman playing a musical instrument was not a typical subject for painting.

The Mandolin Player, by Mary Cassatt

Bacchante , by Mary Cassatt

"The Bacchante" (1872) shows the influence of the great Italian artists. Mary became familiar with them when she went to Parma, Italy, to copy the religious paintings of Corregio for the Bishop of Pittsburgh. Here Mary creates contrast by putting dark shades next to light shades. That contrast gives the woman depth and form. She is not just flat on the canvas.[81] The woman in the painting is wearing clothing that was common in Parma at the time. Mary injected a modern touch by having the woman playing the cymbals. This gives a feeling of motion and activity to the painting.

Bacchante (acc. no: 1932.13.1) Mary Cassatt 1872 Courtesy of the Pennsylvania Academy of Fine Arts, Philadelphia. Gift of John Frederick Lewis

"At the Opera" (1877-1878) shows that Mary was gaining confidence in herself and in her work. In this painting, she seems to have been having fun. She is willing to try something very different. First, Mary chooses an unconventional subject. She chooses a scene from modern life–people attending the theater. More than that, the painting tells a story. The woman in black is using her opera glasses not to look at the performers on stage but to look at something else–or someone else–in the theater. And while she is looking at that unknown thing or person, a man across the way is using his opera glasses to look at her. She, however, seems to be paying no attention to him. The painting seems to suggest that going to the opera was as much about people–watching as it was about the performance itself. It may also suggest that this woman is intent on pursuing her own interests, just as Mary was. The woman in black, sitting alone in the private box, is independent, as Mary was.

At the Opera by Mary Cassatt, 1880
© Burstein Collection/CORBIS

At the Opera by Mary Cassatt

A Cup of Tea by Mary Cassatt

"A Cup of Tea" (1879–1880) shows Mary's focus on home and family. In 1877, Mary's parents and her sister Lydia came to France to live with Mary. Her parents were aging and Lydia was ill. So Mary devoted much time to caring for the three. Her brother Aleck also came with his wife and children to visit. Mary used these family members as models in her paintings. Most often, she used them in painting "slices of home and family life." It was customary for people to have afternoon tea, usually about five o'clock. Friends were always welcome at Mary's home. This painting shows one such afternoon. The silver tea set was a family heirloom. Mary's sister Lydia is having tea with a friend. Notice that the friend is still wearing her hat. That is because afternoon tea did not last more than 15 to 30 minutes. Guests knew they would not be there long. What interested Mary most in these "tea" paintings was the way the people were reacting to one another.[82] Here Lydia seems to be deep in thought, not really paying much attention to her guest. The guest, too, seems to be looking elsewhere, absorbed by something else in the room. Lydia's tea cup is empty. Is that because she's not in the mood for tea or for this guest?

Mary Cassatt and Mary Hillard at Chateau Beaufresne, c.1905 (#290)
Archives, Hill-Stead Museum, Farmington, CT

Opposite:
A Cup of Tea by Mary Cassatt, ca. 1880
© Burstein Collection/CORBIS

"Lydia Seated in the Garden with a Dog in Her Lap" (1880) also shows Mary's focus on home and family. The painting is unconventional in that the figure has her back to the viewer and painter. The woman in the painting is Mary's sister Lydia. She had been very sick, so she may have spent much time sitting quietly in the garden. Surrounded by the beautiful flowers, she is resting comfortably. The dog seems to be a comfort to her. Mary frequently used animals in her paintings.

Mary Cassatt (1844-1926)
Lydia Seated in the Garden with a Dog in Her Lap
Ca. 1880
Oil on convas
10 3/4 x 16 inches
Private collection
Photo courtesy Mary Cassatt Catalogue Raisonné Committee

Lydia Seated in the Garden with a Dog in Her Lap, by Mary Cassatt

Children Playing on the Beach, by Mary Cassatt

"Children Playing on the Beach" (1884) captures another common, everyday subject. That was typical of the Impressionist artists. After her sister Lydia's death in 1882, the family became even more important to Mary. She especially loved to be with her nieces and nephews and other children. In this painting, the children seem to be playing contentedly, ignoring the artist. Mary did not have the children in her paintings pose, as most artists did. She preferred to have her models–especially the children–appear in relaxed, natural positions.[83] Here the children are focused on the pail, shovel, and sand. The children seem to be the image of good health–chubby arms and legs, dimpled elbow, ruddy robust faces. There is no attempt in the painting to make the children appear "cute." The background is vague, so the viewer focuses all attention on the children.

Children Playing on the Beach
1970.17.19.(2391)/PA: Cassatt, Mary
Children Playing on the Beach, Ailas Mellon Bruce Collection, Image © 2004
Board of Trustees, National Gallery of Art, Washington, 1884, oil on canvas,
(38 3/8 x 29 1/4)

"The Child's Bath" (1891) is one of many paintings Mary did of mothers with their children. Though Mary never married and had no children of her own, she is famous for her paintings showing the bond between mother and child. Between 1881 and 1894, Mary did more than 20 mother-and-child pictures in pastels and oils. One reason is that Degas said it was important to paint a single subject over and over again to master it.[84] Another is Mary's experience in Italy. You may recall that when she lived and worked in Italy, she saw many religious paintings of the Madonna and Child. Some people refer to these paintings as Mary Cassatt's "modern madonnas."[85] "The Child's Bath" shows the close bond between mother and child. The child is safe and secure, trusting in her mother's embrace. Both mother and child are concentrating on the same thing. Both are busy washing the child's feet. There is no conflict as there sometimes is between parent and child. Here the eyes of both are focused in the same direction. Both are totally absorbed in the washing of the feet. Even the water pitcher is directed toward the feet in the wash bowl.[86] With everything focused on the feet, the viewer's attention is drawn there too.

Mary Cassatt, American 1844-1926,
The Childs' Bath, 1893, oil on canvas, 39 1/2 x 26 in., Robert A. Waller Fund,
1910.2 Reproduction, The Art Institute of Chicago,
Photography © The Art Institute of Chicago

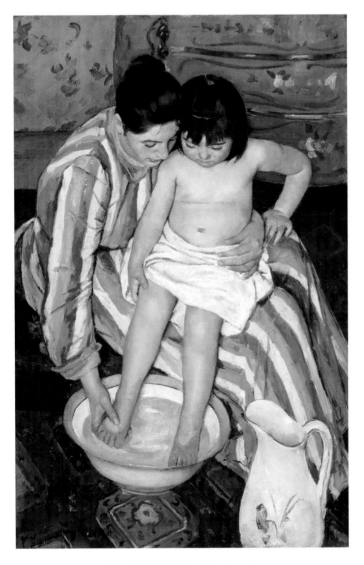

The Child's Bath, by Mary Cassatt

The Boating Party, by Mary Cassatt

"The Boating Party" (1893-1894) puts mother and child in an outdoor setting. The close bond is the same as in Mary's other mother-and-child paintings. Both mother and child here seem to be gazing in the same direction. Unlike most of the other mother-and-child paintings, this one includes a man. But he seems to be outside the bond of the mother and child. Perhaps he owns the boat and is taking the two for a ride. Note that his clothes are dark, in contrast to the mother' and child's clothes. Again, notice the healthy appearance of the child. See how she sits safely in her mother's arms. Mary never tired of showing the strength that women and children derive from the bond they share. [87]

The Boating Party, 1893-1894
Mary Cassatt, The Bridgeman Art Library/Getty Images

"Breakfast in Bed" (1897) conveys a mood, which is characteristic of Impressionistic painting. The puffiness of the pillow, the whiteness of the sheets and nightclothes, and the mother's half-closed eyes create a warm and fuzzy early morning atmosphere. Though she may have had her morning coffee, the woman seems to be taking her time in fully waking and getting up from bed. The child seems to be content, though. Note her crossed legs. She may have a crust of bread in her hand. And she is held snuggly and safely in her mother's embrace. Both carry a healthy glow in their cheeks.

Breakfast in Bed   #83.8.6 Courtesy of the Huntington Library, Collections, and Botanical Gardens, San Marino, California

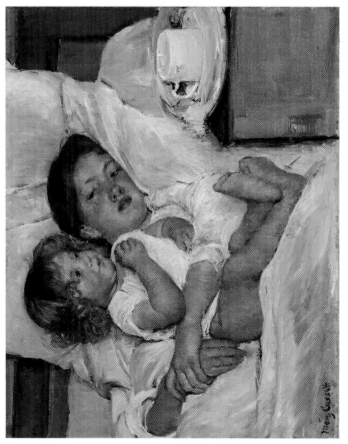

"Breakfast in Bed"

Young Mother Sewing by Mary Cassatt

"Young Mother Sewing" (1900) combines an everyday activity (sewing) with the mother-and-child bond. There are some differences from the other mother-and-child paintings. The closeness is there, but the mother is less focused on the child than on her work. Another difference is that the child is looking boldly right at the viewer. Is she thinking "When will Mom be finished sewing?" Maybe she's thinking: "Well, what are you looking at?"

Young Mother Sewing by Mary Cassatt The Metropolitan Museum of Art, H. O. Havemeyer Collection, Bequest of Mrs. H. O. Havemeyer, 1929. (29.100.48) Photograph © 1997 The Metropolitan Museum of Art

Mary's Timeline

1844   Mary is born in Allegheny City, Pennsylvania.

1851   Mary and her family go to Paris, France. They live there for four years.

1855   The Cassatt family returns to the United States. They live in Philadelphia, then Hollidaysburg, Pennsylvania.

1860   Mary announces that she wants to become an artist.

1860-1864   Mary attends the Pennsylvania Academy of Fine Art.

1865   Mary moves to France to live and study art.

1867   Mary submits a painting to the Salon. It is rejected.

1868   Mary submits "The Mandolin Player" to the Salon under the name of Mary Stevenson. It is accepted.

1870   The Franco-Prussian war erupts; Mary returns to the United States.

1871   Mary goes to Parma, Italy to paint copies of Corregio paintings for the Bishop of Pittsburgh.

1872   Mary goes to Spain to live and study in Madrid and Seville.

1873   Mary's "Offering the Panale to the Toreador" is accepted at the Salon.

1874   Edgar Degas founds the group called "Independents," later called the "Impressionists." Degas sees Mary's painting "Ida" and invites Mary to join the Impressionist group.

1877   Mary's parents and her sister Lydia come to live with her in France. Mary's nieces and nephew spend the summer there with her. Mary uses her family members as models in her paintings.

1879   Eleven of Mary's paintings are displayed at the Hall of the Rejected exhibit. Her paintings earn her $100.00 and high critical praise.

1880   (*and following*)   Mary produces many paintings. Her reputation spreads and she sells many paintings. Mary also devotes much time to caring for her ailing sister Lydia and aging parents.

1881   (*and following*)   Mary paints 20 mother-and-child canvases, among others.

1882 Lydia dies of kidney disease.

1886 Mary helps organize Hall of the Rejected exhibit and helps other artists display and sell their work. She becomes trusted advisor to art collectors.

1891 Mary's father dies.

1892 Mary paints "Modern Woman" mural for World's Columbian Exposition in Chicago.

1895 Mary's mother dies.

1895 (*and following*) Mary uses "Modern Woman" mural as basis for many other works on the role of women. Her fame and success continue to grow.

1911 Mary's failing eyesight keeps her from painting.

1914-1918 World War I rages in Europe. Mary sees the need for women to vote.

1915 Mary's work is displayed and sold in the Suffrage Benefit Exhibition in New York to raise money to be used in campaign for women's right to vote.

1920 Women in the United States gain the right to vote.

1926 Mary dies at age 82.

Endnotes

1 Tom Streissguth. *Mary Cassatt: Portrait of an American Impressionist*. Carolrhoda Books Inc. Minneapolis, 1999, page 8.

2 Streissguth, p. 7.

3 Nicolas Pioch. *Mary Cassatt*. http://www.biblio.org/wm/paint/auth/Cassatt,webmuseum,Paris.

4 Streissguth, p. 9.

5 Nancy Mowll Mathews, ed. *Cassatt and Her Circle: Selected Letters*. Abbeville Press, NY, 1984, p. 12.

6 Streissguth, pp. 15-16.

7 Robyn Montana Turner. *Mary Cassatt: Portraits of Women Artists for Children series*. Little, Brown & Company, Toronto, 1992, p. 8.

8 Streissguth, pp. 16-19.

9 Mathews, p. 16.

10 Streissguth, p. 21.

11 Catalogue right frame. http://www.metmueseum.org/explore/cassatt/html/life.

12 Streissguth, p. 26.

13 Matthews, p. 18.

14 Streissguth, p. 27.

15 Mathews, p. 93.

16 Catalogue right frame, p.1.

17 Streissguth, pp. 44-45.

18 Mathews, p. 281.

19 Streissguth, pp. 28-29.

20 Turner, p. 10.

21 Mathews, p. 75.

22 Matthews, p. 70.

23 Streissguth, p. 30.

24 Philip Brooks. *Mary Cassatt: An American in Paris*. Franklin Watts, NY, 1995, pp. 30-31.

25 Streissguth, pp. 31-32.

26 Matthews, p. 66.

27 Streissguth, p. 32.

28 Brooks, pp. 31-32.

29 Mathews, p. 103.

30 Streissguth, p. 36.

31 Brooks, p. 32.

32 Richard Muhlberg. *What Makes a Cassatt a Cassatt?* The Metropolitan Museum of Art, New York, 1994, p. 11.

33 Streissguth, pp. 38-39.

34 *"Mary Cassatt: Modern Woman."* Art Institute of Chicago. www.tfaoi.com/newsmu/nmus1dhtm.

35 Brooks, p. 36.

36 Artelino-Art Auctions. http://www.artelino.com/articles/mary_cassatt.asp.

37 Streissguth, p. 42.

38 Brooks, pp. 34-35.

39 *"The Life and Times of Mary Cassatt."* http://www.devine-ent.com/shows/artists/cassatt-bio.shtml.

40 Turner, p. 14.

41 Catalogue right frame, p. 2.'

42 Streissguth, pp.42-43.

43 *"Women of the Hall."* National Women's Hall of Fame. http://www.great-women.org/women.

44 Catalogue right frame, p. 1.

45 Web museum, p. 1.

46 Streissguth, p. 49.

47 Artelino, p. 1.

48 Brooks, p. 44.

49 Streissguth, p. 54.

50 Mathews, p. 136.

51 Pioch, Nicolas. WebMuseum, Paris.
http://www.biblio.org/wm/paint/auth/Cassatt.

52 Streissguth, pp. 37-38.

53 Griselda Pollock. *Mary Cassatt: Painter of Modern Women.* Thanes and
Hudson, Lt. London, 1998, p. 36.

54 Pollock, p. 38.

55 Streissguth, p. 87.

56 Pollock, p. 41.

57 Matthews, p. 238.

58 Muhlberg, p. 36.

59 Mathews, p. 242.

60 Pollock, p. 43.

61 Muhlberg, p. 36.

62 Pollock, p. 47.

63 Pollock, p. 40.

64 Matthews, p. 271.

65 Pollock, p. 27.

66 Matthews, p. 323.

67 Mathews, p. 271.

68 Mathews, p. 321.

69 Streissguth, p. 102.

70 Mathews, pp. 159-60.

71 Mathews, pp. 156-157.

72 Turner, p. 16.

73 Mathews, p. 211.

74 Matthews, pp. 117-118.

75 Mathews, p. 12.

76 Mathews, p. 13.

77 *"Mary Cassatt Quotes." Women's Voices: Quotations by Women.*
http://womenshistory. About.com/library/qu/blqucass.htm

78 Streissguth, p. 52.

79 Mathews, p. 11.

80 "The Permanent Collection." National Museum of Women in the Arts. Mary Cassatt. http://www.nmwa.org/collection/profile. .asp?LinkID-128.

81 Turner, p. 10.

82 Muhlberg, p. 23.

83 Turner, p. 18.

84 MSC, p. 1.

85 MSC, p. 2.

86 Turner, p. 28.

87 Art Institute of Chicago, p. 23.

References

Artelino-Art Auctions. http://www.artelino.com/articles/mary_cassatt.asp.

Brooks, Philip. *Mary Cassatt: An American in Paris*. Franklin Watts, NY, 1995.

Cassatt, Mary. http://www.encyclopedia.com/html/c/cassatt.asp.

Catalogue right frame. http://www.metmueseum.org/explore/cassatt/html/life.

The Collection: National Gallery of Art. http://www.nga.gov/collection/gallery/ggcassattptg/ggcassattptg-over1.html.

"The Life and Times of Mary Cassatt." http://www.devine-ent.com/shows/artists/cassatt-bio.shtml.

Mary Cassatt: American Impressionist. http://www.devine-ent.com/shows/artists/cassatt-synopsis.shtml.

"Mary Cassatt: Modern Woman." Art Institute of Chicago. www.tfaoi.com/newsmu/nmus1dhtm.

"Mary Cassatt Quotes." Women's Voices: Quotations by Women. http://womenshistory.about.com/library/qu/blqucass.htm.

Mary Stevenson Cassatt. http://www.butlerart.com/pc_book/pages/mary_stevenson_cassatt_1845.htm.

Matthews, Nancy Mowll, ed. *Cassatt and Her Circle: Selected Letters*. Abbeville Press, NY, 1984.

Muhlberg, Richard. *What Makes a Cassatt a Cassatt?* The Metropolitan Museum of Art, New York, 1994.

"The Permanent Collection." National Museum of Women in the Arts. Mary Cassatt. http://www.nmwa.org/collection/profile.asp?LinkID-128.

Pioch, Nicolas. WebMuseum, Paris. http://www.biblio.org/wm/paint/auth/Cassatt.

Pollock, Griselda. *Mary Cassatt: Painter of Modern Women*. Thanes and Hudson, Lt. London, 1998.

Streissguth, Tom. *Mary Cassatt: Portrait of an American Impressionist.*
   Carolrhoda Books Inc. Minneapolis, 1999.

Turner, Robyn Montana. *Mary Cassatt: Portraits of Women Artists for Children
   series.* Little, Brown & Company, Toronto, 1992.

Who Is Mary Cassatt? http://www.users.totalise.co.uk/tmd/mary-cassatt.htm.

"Women of the Hall." National Women's Hall of Fame.
   http://www.greatwomen.org/women.

"Wonderful Things Inside." Mary Cassatt. http://www.3Dmart.org.image.pl.